E. Bergman

SHARAKU

MASTERWORKS OF UKIYO-E

SHARAKU

by Jūzō Suzuki

translation by John Bester

KODANSHA INTERNATIONAL LTD.
Tokyo, New York and San Francisco

Distributors:
UNITED STATES: *Harper & Row, Publishers, Inc., 10 East 53rd Street, New York, New York 10022.* SOUTH AMERICA: *Harper & Row, International Department.* CANADA: *Fitzhenry & Whiteside Limited, 150 Lesmill Road, Don Mills, Ontario.* MEXICO & CENTRAL AMERICA: *HARLA S. A. de C. V., Apartado 30–546, Mexico 4, D. F.* BRITISH COMMONWEALTH *(excluding Canada & the Far East):* TABS, *7 Maiden Lane, London WC2.* EUROPE: *Boxerbooks Inc., Limmatstrasse 111, 8031 Zurich.* AUSTRALIA & NEW ZEALAND: *Book Wise (Australia) Pty. Ltd., 104–8 Sussex Street, Sydney.* THAI-LAND: *Central Department Store Ltd., 306 Silom Road, Bangkok.* HONG KONG & SINGAPORE: *Books for Asia Ltd., 30 Tat Chee Avenue, Kowloon; 65 Crescent Road, Singapore 15.* THE FAR EAST: *Japan Publications Trading Company, P.O. Box 5030, Tokyo International, Tokyo.*

Published by Kodansha International Ltd., 2-12-21 Otowa, Bunkyo-ku, Tokyo 112 and Kodansha International/USA, Ltd., 10 East 53rd Street, New York, New York 10022 and 44 Montgomery Street, San Francisco, California 94104. Copyright © 1969 by Kodansha International Ltd. All rights reserved. Printed in Japan.

LCC 68–13470
ISBN 0–87011–056–x
JBC 0371–780553–2361

First edition, 1968
Third printing, 1975

Contents

Translator's Preface

THERE IS a special fascination in the great artist of the past whose person is as elusive and enigmatic as his art is substantial and unequivocal. In the West, Shakespeare is perhaps the outstanding example; in Japan, Sharaku. Shadowy against the colorful backdrop of Elizabethan and Jacobean London, Shakespeare has always been a challenge to the amateur of literary detection. Even more challenging, however, is the figure of Sharaku, of whom almost nothing is known apart from the fact that all his extant work was done in the years 1794 and 1795.

About his times and environment, however, we know even more than in Shakespeare's case. The city of Edo—the city that, under its modern name of Tokyo, was to become the world's largest—already had a population of over a million. It was a city with a complex, organized life of its own. The presence of the shogun, Japan's de facto ruler, made it the true center of the national life in a way impossible for the old capital of Kyoto, where a court of puppets occupied itself with outdated rituals. And the presence of the Edo residences of feudal lords, who were obliged to visit the city regularly and brought with them large numbers of their servants and retainers, helped bring the city new wealth.

It was a city of wooden or clay walls and tiled roofs; of great samurai mansions, wealthy merchant residences, and the hovels of the poor; of theaters and temples, bathhouses and brothels; a city, above all, that by Sharaku's time had enjoyed close on two centuries of peace and relative prosperity, marred only by recurrent fires and earthquakes.

The peace had been obtained only at a price. Just as the shogun's castle, the headquarters of the ruling Tokugawa clan, with its great complex of moats and ramparts, dominated the city physically, so the need of that clan to perpetuate its own rule placed a restraining hand on the lives of all who were subject to it. A reign that had begun in 1603 and was to last until the opening of the country to the West and the "restoration" of the emperor in 1868 could only be maintained by strict preservation of a caste system that divided society up into four classes—the samurai, the merchants, the artisans, and the farmers. And in the great commercial center that Edo had become, the fact that the machinery of government was almost exclusively in the hands of the samurai, whereas trade—and, increasingly, wealth—was in the hands of the merchants was also of the greatest significance culturally.

The samurai class had its own traditional culture. Thus it patronized the Nō—the classical theater which had come into being in the fifteenth century—and, in the field of painting, conservative schools such as the Tosa and the Kanō. The samurai also made innovations, of course, and men of samurai birth were to be responsible for new developments in the arts. In time, moreover, there was a certain amount of overlapping with the merchant class, so that it became increasingly difficult to label some forms of art either as "samurai" or as "merchant." Even so, it was natural that the merchants and artisans, whose lives were so different from those of the samurai, should seek some genuine means of self-expression of their own. They were clearly energetic. What was more, being in many cases relatively well fed, well clothed, and well housed, they had energy to spare.

The question was, where to find suitable outlets for that energy. They were restricted physically by living in an island nation cut off by its own government from the outside world and divided by feudal barriers. Spiritually, they were hampered by a regime watchful of any threat to its security, by the class barriers that cut them off from, say a political career, and by the systems of human relationships imposed by official Confucian ethics.

Small wonder, then, that their wealth and energies should find outlets in a love of extravagance which the sumptuary edicts of an anxious shogunate failed to suppress; in a preoccupation with their own everyday lives rather than any larger issues; and in an extraordinary zeal in the pursuit of pleasure. Thus there was an enormous output of popular literature—humorous, ironic, and erotic—dealing with the lives, the loves, and the scandals of the common people. The kabuki, the popular theater which had already produced many major playwrights, was largely concerned—when it was not indulging in historical romancing—with the sensations and tensions of the Edoite's own society. The gay quarters, seen through a glamorous haze, provided an outlet for pent-up romanticism, and a setting where the male could test his masculinity and his sense of style at the same time.

Artistically speaking, however, the most important development of all was the emergence of the woodcut print. The type of picture known as ukiyo-e—literally, "floating world picture," since it drew its subjects

8

largely from the more hedonistic and ephemeral aspects of contemporary society—came increasingly to be associated with the print form, and the single-sheet print, which first came into its own in the latter half of the seventeenth century, quite naturally found two of its most frequent sources of inspiration in the theater and the gay quarters. As objects of popular adulation, the great courtesans and leading kabuki actors could rival any of the idols of today. The great difference lies, however, in the extraordinary quality of the art which they inspired and which—still more extraordinarily—was the everyday fare of a large section of the plebeian public.

With the development of the polychrome print from the mid-eighteenth century on, the form enjoyed a kind of golden age. The list of first-ranking ukiyo-e artists who were alive in those two years during which Sharaku produced his work is a formidable one, including as it does Katsukawa Shunshō (1726–92), Katsukawa Shun'ei (1768–1819), Utagawa Toyoharu (1735–1814), Torii Kiyonaga (1752–1815), Kitagawa Utamaro (1753–1806), Utagawa Toyokuni (1769–1825), and Katsushika Hokusai (1760–1849). Their work, done sometimes for a publisher, sometimes as a result of a private commission, involved the closest collaboration among the artist who did the original design, the engraver, and the printer, and the publisher's job lay largely in getting together groups of men who could do good teamwork.

Sharaku himself must have been one of such a team, for a short period at least. And the fact that the society of artists, literati, and publishers in which he must have moved was comparatively small and had a keen ear for gossip makes it all the more surprising, as Mr. Suzuki points out, that more mention is not made of him by his contemporaries. In fact, all that we know for sure of his life can be summed up in two or three lines.

It is typical of Mr. Suzuki's painstaking scholarship that he does not attempt to eke out fact with imagination. For the scholar, he clears the ground, sums up the facts, and adds something new of his own. For the general reader, he describes the extent and nature of Sharaku's oeuvre, and suggests where its greatness lies. Most important of all, he has assembled in one volume the largest and most wide-ranging collection of color reproductions of Sharaku's work yet to appear. It makes one feel still more strongly that Sharaku's work was a truly extraordinary achievement for a period of only a few months; and still more it makes one regret that knowledge of that lonely figure who moved briefly across the colorful scene of eighteenth-century Edo is, in all likelihood, forever beyond our grasp.

J.B.

Sharaku

IN ARTISTIC and theatrical circles, there is a tendency to exaggerate and embellish the more out-of-the-ordinary words and deeds of celebrated figures, and to serve them up in distorted forms calculated to glamorize the artists' works or performances and induce appropriate feelings of reverence in the layman.

The world of ukiyo-e was no stranger to this tendency. A well-known story, for example, tells how the great artist Hokusai's almost willfully stubborn insistence on his own views led him into collision with, and estrangement from, the novelist Bakin, a man known for his arrogance. Even Hiroshige, mild, considerate man though he was, is said to have been driven by the creative impulse to leave home without a word to his family and, still in his everyday attire, to have embarked on a journey which took him all the way south to Shikoku—whence, it is said, he returned after many a month, only to sit down at his desk and produce his great work depicting the whirlpools of Naruto. And one commonly hears other tales similarly eulogizing the so-called artistic temperament.

It is equally common, however, if one takes the trouble to inquire into the foundations which these anecdotes have in objective fact, to discover that those foundations are, after all, either shaky or a mass of contradictions. The tale of Hokusai and Bakin's quarrel is a case in point. In the first place, several products of their collaboration survive from dates after that at which they are supposed to have split. More conclusive still, there survives a record in which Bakin himself gives a detailed account of how, as a result of some personal friction, he and Hokusai ceased having their joint works published by the firm which had hitherto handled them—a story which was obviously distorted in the telling until it emerged as the present tale of a tiff between Bakin and Hokusai over artistic matters. With Hiroshige too, an examination of the dates on the seals attached to his extant works will show that during the year or so preceding publication of his celebrated "Naruto Whirlpool" triptych, he was busy with his "Hundred Famous

Sights in Edo" and other series, and it is extremely unlikely that he embarked on any long journey.

Despite the unreliability of such popular traditions, most laymen tend—or rather, prefer—to swallow them almost unconditionally. The effect that can be produced by such later fabrications working on the general Japanese fondness for an Oriental-style, misty-eyed approach to celebrity, and the average layman's weakness for a good journalistic story is not to be underestimated. Nor should one underestimate its power to distort academic truth. For such reasons, I have always tried, in discussing the ukiyo-e artists, to avoid subjective judgments and unquestioning acceptance of popular traditions, and to assemble the contemporary, objective evidence concerning the artist in question, relating it to his work in the hope that some image of the artist as a man will emerge.

Unfortunately, to apply this same methodology to Tōshūsai Sharaku, one of the greatest figures in the whole history of the ukiyo-e, is to find oneself up against a formidable barrier. The basic sources on which one should rely for the elementary facts of his life are as good as non-existent, nor is any satisfactory circumstantial evidence at hand to take its place. Although the popular writers and artists of Edo formed a comparatively close-knit society, and often shared the same publishers or did work together, well-known literary contemporaries are distressingly unhelpful. The diligent writing brush of Bakin has left us not a single reminiscence. In vain does one thumb the pages of the humorous novelettes of Santō Kyōden for any character inspired by Sharaku—whom one would have expected Kyōden to come across, on a few occasions at least, at Tsutaya, the publisher who handled both men's work. The prolific novelist Jippensha Ikku, and Shikitei Samba, a humorous writer with a love for historical research, do at least corroborate the existence of such a print artist among their contemporaries (see pages 17 and 21), but with tantalizing insouciance confine themselves to the briefest of hints at the existence of a man about whom they could presumably have told so much more. Even the satirical novelist and poet Ōta Nampo, who of all the figures of his day would seem most qualified in knowledge and background to speak for Sharaku, and who himself owned some of Sharaku's prints, actually stamping them with his own private seal (see *Japanese Prints, Sharaku to Toyokuni, in the collection of Louis V. Ledoux,* 1950), dismisses him with a curt line or so in the *Ukiyo-e Ruikō,* a work which he compiled himself (see page 17). Indeed, the literary and artistic figures of the day might almost have been ostracizing Sharaku, or deliberately giving him a wide berth, so unanimous is their silence concerning his career. It was because of this silence that the theory that Sharaku was in the service of the Lord of Awa as one of a troupe of Nō actors captured the imaginations of scholars when it first became current around the end of the Edo period, and overready acceptance of it has led to some extravagant flights of fancy.

"The reason why Sharaku gave up pictures after so short a time," one of the grand old men of ukiyo-e studies told me over dinner, with apparently complete confidence, "was that he was a Nō actor in the service of a daimyo (feudal lord) family, the Hachisukas. He was officially rebuked for unseemly conduct in having done pictures of kabuki actors—who were little better than outcasts, you see—and was packed off home to Awa."

For a moment, my skepticism wavered: after all, such a thing was quite likely in a feudal society with a strict social hierarchy and a strong class consciousness. Yet still my mind balked at unqualified acceptance, and I tried checking the Hachisuka family archives and other sources to determine the movements of Haruaki, head of the Hachisuka family, around 1794–5. These documents showed that the daimyo in question arrived in Edo on the sixth of the fourth month of 1793, and left for home on the twenty-first of the fourth month of 1794; he next arrived in Edo on the second of the fourth month of 1796.

Assuming that the Nō actors in his service accompanied their master on his journeys, this would mean that Sharaku was not in Edo during the period when he is believed to have produced his prints—that is, from the fifth month of 1794 to the first month of 1795. The old gentleman's theory would still hold water, of course, if the actors were stationed permanently in Edo. The fact remains, however, that no positive identification of Sharaku with the Nō actor in the service of the Lord of Awa can be made until such time as some incontrovertible contemporary evidence comes to light. Such sources on the Awa side as I have turned up offer no clue whatsoever, and the barrier remains as opaque as ever.

Perhaps—I told myself—one might be able to uncover something by research in the field of the kabuki, the world which Sharaku portrayed through his art. Here again, though, my efforts came up against a formidable barrier. Investigation would have been easy enough with plays which received frequent performances. In fact, though, a majority of the pieces which inspired Sharaku's prints were written to order for the occasions, and their librettos have vanished into oblivion. Thus the only possibility left was to rely on the various printed programs (*banzuke*) of the time—pamphlets and single sheets—which still survive. These include the *yakuwari banzuke* (programs giving the cast of a play; also known as *mon* or "crest" *banzuke* because the crests of the actors were printed on the cover; they were printed as soon as the casting was decided and contained no pictures), the *ehon banzuke* ("picture-book programs";

also known as *e* or "picture" *banzuke;* these included pictures of important scenes), and the *tsuji banzuke* ("crossroad programs," i.e. for use as posters providing publicity before the season started). To these must be added accounts of the plays found in contemporary comments on the actors and their performances. All these I used to gain some idea of the outlines of the plays involved, and of their relevance to the works of Sharaku.

It was a frustrating method that never allowed one to get to close grips with the subject, but it yielded at least a certain amount of results. It would have been overoptimistic, of course, to hope for any finds such as would upset established theory, but nevertheless I discovered a few *ehon banzuke* and *yakuwari banzuke* which made possible some minor additions and amendments to that theory, and which may contribute in some measure to future studies too. I feel that if only one could find out a little more about the scenes Sharaku chose to illustrate and the performance of the actors concerned, and consider them analytically, one would gain some hint at least of the interests and impulses that moved this supremely enigmatic artist.

As for the position of Sharaku's work in relation to the general development of the actor-picture—from the intellectualized depictions of the Torii school, through the realistic likenesses of the Katsukawa school, and on to the Utagawa school with its fondness for sensuous pictures from life—I shall have more to say later. The most important thing in discussing his career and artistic outlook as revealed in his work is not to give way to the temptations of the fancy. Julius Kurth, who first introduced the artist in the West, presented him in his book *Sharaku* as a Nō actor dwelling amidst the wonders of nature in the province of Awa. Under the spell cast by Sharaku's work, his prose soars on the wings of fancy, and the reader finds himself carried away in spite of himself. Nevertheless, work on Sharaku today, when studies have in many respects advanced beyond the point at which they stood in Dr. Kurth's day, should be based on a sounder and more strictly scholarly analysis of the available sources of information.

There are various other examples of the fatal fascination of the subject. A fictional account of how Sharaku, incurring the hatred of theater people and their patrons, was set on one night and lost his right arm to the sword was embodied in an interesting work, *Tōshūsai Sharaku,* by the late Kunieda Kanji. More recently, a play on a similar theme, *Sharaku, Ukiyo-e Artist,* was presented at a theater in Tokyo, and the same theme occurred again in a short story, *Sharaku's Arm,* by Kon Tōkō.

The creative writer is, of course, free to use his imagination in a work of art, and his public is free to enjoy the results, but it scarcely needs pointing out that, once one enters the field of research, one's mental slate must be wiped quite clean of all basically untenable hypotheses before one can begin work. With Sharaku, the available sources are so meager that one is often tempted into rash hypotheses out of sheer frustration. Nevertheless, the only valid method remains to go back personally to the materials used by previous students, in their original forms, and to evolve one's own method of study based on the evidence of one's own eyes. The process is tedious, yet may well yield unexpected scraps of information that pave the way for future advances. That was the idea with which I set about the research on which this brief essay is based.

At the beginning of the next section, I have dwelt on the work of my predecessors at some length because I wanted first of all to define the extent of the ground already covered. All I have done is to start to set forth an approach which I have long been wanting to apply to Sharaku studies. More satisfying to me personally, in fact, was the chance to assemble in one volume color reproductions of many works which have never been seen together before—and for this I am indebted to all those whose understanding and aid have made this book possible. I am delighted that my ukiyo-e studies have, incidentally, made it possible for me to present in this form the works of such an artist. I can only urge the reader to look at the works themselves as they appear here, and to experience for himself the wonder of Sharaku's art.

FIRST DISCOVERY AND SUBSEQUENT STUDIES

Today, the world agrees in ranking Sharaku's achievement among the very highest. Yet in the embryo period of ukiyo-e studies—around the time, in the late 1890's and 1900's, when the American art critic Ernest Fenollosa was first beginning to introduce the ukiyo-e to a worldwide public—it still seems to have attracted comparatively little attention, even among educated Japanese. For Fenollosa himself, who measured everything against the yardstick of a typically "Japanese"—i.e. an unemphatic, harmonious—beauty, the ferociously expressive work of Sharaku could not fail to appear an unsightly intruder among a well-bred company (though Sharaku's prints had, incidentally, by that time won the high opinion of discerning Frenchmen). If even Fenollosa—the man credited with fostering a true understanding of Japanese art in Japan as well as abroad—remained indifferent, was it to be expected that Sharaku should find readier understanding among others? Thus even Miyatake Tobone (Gaikotsu), one of the greatest early champions of ukiyo-e, could write in 1910, a propos of a portrait of the actor Ichikawa Ebizō:

"Mica-dust background. Sharaku seems to have had no

particular master. He produced a droll kind of portrait reminiscent of Jichōsai of Osaka. Many people express wonder that foreigners will happily pay several dozen yen for a single copy of this print. I myself have no inclination to pay high prices for such stuff, and make do with a collection of the copies put out by Kōkodō in Tokyo."

At the same time, the very fact that reproductions of Sharaku were being produced in Japan suggests that his work was already achieving a corresponding popularity, among foreigners at least. In fact, appreciation of the ukiyo-e abroad around this time had far outstripped that in Japan. The catalog for an auction of works in the possession of Hayashi Tadamasa, published in Paris in 1902, lists 24 prints by Sharaku, while the Barboutau catalog issued in 1904 made an even braver showing, with 16 prints by Sharaku reproduced in collotype, as well as eight works claimed to be original drawings for actor-pictures. It was this same popularity which inspired *Sharaku*, that epoch-making study of the artist by Julius Kurth, and it is an ironical fact that 1910, the year of the publication of this work, was the same year that saw Miyatake's chilly dismissal. Kurth's work touched off a series of articles dealing with Sharaku in Japanese art magazines during the 1910's, and investigation into his work and life gradually stepped up. One of the first full-length books on the subject was Nakada Katsunosuke's *Sharaku* (1925), followed in 1930 by Noguchi Yonejirō's *Tōshūsai Sharaku*. With Rumpf's *Sharaku* (1932), the public was given a more or less dependable summing-up of all that was known at the time. In Japan, the late Inoue Kazuo published in periodicals the results of his work in identifying the kabuki roles portrayed in the prints. *The Surviving Works of Sharaku* by Henderson and Ledoux (1939), was a fine achievement, the result of a far-reaching search for sources, together with help given by Ihara Toshio and Kimura Sutezō with research into the names of roles and actors. With these works, most of the basic work in study was done, though our knowledge advanced another step—or rather, several steps— by Yoshida Teruji's *Tōshūsai Sharaku* (1943), published after the war in a revised and enlarged edition entitled *Sharaku* (1956).

To apply my own small spade to a patch of earth already so thoroughly worked over may seem superfluous. Yet if one digs in the right way, one may still find small supplementary pieces of information which will be of reference value in the future.

THE IMPENETRABLE VEIL
Investigation of Sharaku's life, wrapped as it is in an impenetrable veil that has left us almost totally ignorant of even the most elementary facts, has

16

long been fast stuck in the mud. There is no progress; if anything, the perplexity deepens still further. The real trouble, of course, lies in the lack of basic source materials. At the same time, I cannot help feeling that the situation is due in part to an approach that neglects a bibliographical scrutiny of the materials already available and a thorough examination of their credentials and their reliability. For example, the *Ukiyo-e Ruikō* mentioned above is considered one of the basic sources of information, but since we do not have the original, scholars have had to rely on transcriptions. There are, in fact, many different versions of it, such as the *Zoku* (Revised) *Ukiyo-e Ruikō*, *Zōho* (Enlarged) *Ukiyo-e Ruikō*, and the *Shin Zōho* (New Enlarged) *Ukiyo-e Ruikō*, in which later hands have made wholesale additions and omissions. To treat all these later variations of equal value, without distinguishing among them according to the time when they were made and the sources on which they drew, is likely to lead the student astray; to take only one example, the theory that Sharaku was a Nō actor does not appear in the *Ukiyo-e Ruikō* in its original form, but in a transcription of a later period. It will be worth the trouble, therefore, of setting forth chronologically the references to Sharaku made in the various versions of the *Ukiyo-e Ruikō*, and giving them some reconsideration.

1. *Ukiyo-e Ruikō* (the original, compiled by Ōta Nampo with additions by Sasaya Kuninori during the Kansei era (1789–1801), is lost, and we must rely on a copy dated 1831):

> "Sharaku: Another artist who did likenesses of actors, but his excess of zeal to draw the real realistically led him to produce strange works, so that his popularity did not last long, and he ceased work within a year or two."

2. The addition in the version of the same work transcribed by Katō Eibian:

> "Nevertheless, he is worthy of praise for the stylishness of his line."

3. Additions to the same work made by Shikitei Samba (included with the copy of the 1831 version):

> "Note by Samba: Sharaku, artistic name Tōshūsai, dwelt in Hatchōbori, Edo, was popular for only half a year."

4. *Mumei-ō Zuihitsu* ("Essays by a Nameless Old Man," also known as *Zoku Ukiyo-e Ruikō*, compiled by Keisai Eisen. No good copy being available, I quoted from the copy in the National Diet Library):

> "Did likenesses of actors . . . " (what follows is essentially the same as (1) and (3) above, but continues—) "did half-length portraits of actors such as Hakuen V., Koshirō (later Kyōjurō), Hanshirō, Kikunojō, Tomijūrō, Hiroji, Sukegorō, Oniji, and Nakazō."

It is usual to follow these quotations with one from the *Shin Zōho Ukiyo-e Ruikō*, but I feel that it is necessary, instead, to introduce here some passages from the *Zōho Ukiyo-e Ruikō* which have not been quoted hitherto.

5. *Zōho Ukiyo-e Ruikō* (In the Cambridge University Library, written personally by Saitō Gesshin, a district headman in Edo and a student of history.) The material was reproduced in Nos. II and III of *Kinsei Bungei Shiryō to Kōshō* ("Sources and Studies in Edo Period Literature"):

> "Sharaku: A figure of the Temmei (1781–88) and Kansei eras, original name Saitō Jūrōbei, dwelt in Hatchōbori, Edo. A Nō actor in the troupe of the Lord of Awa . . . " (what follows is essentially the same as (1), (3), and (4) above) " . . . frequently used mica dust for his backgrounds."

6. *Shin Zōho Ukiyo-e Ruikō* (the version with insertions by Kawasaki Chitora in the National Diet Library, with a preface by Tatsutaya Shūkin dated 1868). In its content, the passage is identical with that in (5), except that this time the name "Nakazō" is placed before "Tomijūrō" in the list of actors.

7. *Ihon Ukiyo-e Ruikō* (quoted in Nakada Katsunosuke's *Sharaku*):

> "Also called himself Sharakusai. Managed a bookstore in Yokkaichi and wrote plays on the side. Died at the age of 48 in the intercalary first month of 1822."

8. *Nogi Katei-bon Ukiyo-e Ruikō* (discussed by Inoue Kazuo in No. 8 of the journal *Ukiyo-e*). To the entry on Sharaku is appended the following passage:

> "Won renown in his day with his portraits of actors; was also good at oil painting. Artistic name was Yūrin. Died in 1801."

Let us begin now by eliminating those of the just-quoted sources which seem to be either mistaken or doubtful. First, there is (7). Harry Packard, an enthusiastic student of Sharaku, has recently, with considerable perspicacity, pointed to the possibility of a passage relating to Shikitei Samba—who died in the year cited here, and used the same pseudonymn as Sharaku—having crept into the account of Sharaku by mistake. This suggests to me that the passage is derived from a work about the writers of popular novelettes in Edo entitled *Gesaku Rokka-sen* ("Six Selected Popular Novelists") written by Iwamoto Kattōshi in 1856. Just how it happened is not clear, but the probability of confusion having occurred seems great.

Where (8) is concerned, the passage in question is found in an insertion in a version of the *Ukiyo-e Ruikō* which was in the possession of Yaboku Katei, also known as Ōgusa Kinsuke, a retainer of the shogunate and student of history. However, the book which the late Inoue Kazuo relied on in his article was a later transcription of the original (see *Ukiyo-e* No. 48, June 1919). Accordingly (since the fate of the original is unknown), it is impossible to tell whether the insertion was made by the original author or the man who made the transcription, and it would seem safer for the moment to set the passage aside as unconfirmed evidence.

We are left with (1) – (6) as evidence for our study—which means in practice (1) – (5), since (6) is included within (5). Let us use these as a basis for a brief chronological survey of what was said about Sharaku throughout the years.

The *Ukiyo-e Ruikō* as it was originally compiled during the Kansei era, in which Sharaku was still alive, confines itself to the vaguest outline: Sharaku had tried to be so true to life in his portraits of actors that he had gone to unpleasant extremes, had proved unpopular as a result, and had had a productive life of a mere year or two. However, by the end of the Bunka era (1804–17), when Katō Eibian transcribed the *Ukiyo-e Ruikō*, there were people who considered that Sharaku had a "stylish line." Next, when Shikitei Samba made additions around the Bunsei era (1818–30), he provided the supplementary information that Sharaku had lived in the Hatchōbori district of Edo. In the following Tempō era (1830–44), Keisai Eisen, in his "Essays of a Nameless Old Man," added some research on the actors whom Sharaku had portrayed. Unfortunately, his conclusions are suspect since Tomijūrō, Hiroji, and Sukegorō are not found among Sharaku's half-length portraits of actors.

The account by Gesshin in the *Zōho Ukiyo-e Ruikō* both helps and propounds new questions. This is the earliest work we have at the moment that states that Sharaku's original name was Saitō Jūrōbei, or that he was a Nō actor in the service of the Lord of Awa. Since the work is in Gesshin's own hand, there is no possibility that the passages are insertions by a later hand. In the past, the fact that no mention is made in the reproductions of the *Zōho Ukiyo-e Ruikō* in general circulation of the theory that Sharaku was a Nō actor named Saitō Jūrōbei has been taken as proof that the note to this effect first turned up in (6), the *Shin Zōho Ukiyo-e Ruikō*. Similarly, the theory that the artist was a Nō actor in the service of the Lord of Awa— which had received general credence because of the fact that the Hatchōbori mentioned by Samba as Sharaku's place of residence was in fact the site of the Edo residence of the Hachisuka family, hereditary lords of Awa— had been viewed with skepticism by the late Kondō Ichitarō because of the excessive gap in time between Sharaku's lifetime and the date when the *Shin Zōho Ukiyo-e Ruikō* came into being. Now, however, with the appearance of the Gesshin version of the work, the Saitō Jūrōbei and Nō actor theories can be traced back at least as far as 1844 when Gesshin wrote.

Not of course that this immediately serves to upset Professor Kondō's theories; the interval between the Kansei and Kōka eras is still great, and the evidence is too weak to be decisive. Nor do we have any knowledge of the grounds Gesshin had for his supposition.

Is there, then, any evidence that there really was an actor named Saitō Jūrōbei? In this connection, I have unearthed a few more shreds of evidence. As long ago as 1930, it was reported that one Mori Keisuke living in Tokushima Prefecture was in possession of a Nō program of 1824 in which this very name appeared. Then recently, Mr. Kōno Tarō of Tokushima University informed me that among the records of "Proceedings Marking the Change of Office of Lord Ienari and the Assumption of Additional Office by Lord Ieyoshi" (i.e. the retirement of one Tokugawa shogun and his replacement by another) in the *Records of Tokugawa Ceremonies*, there was a still older Nō program for the fifteenth of the fourth month, 1816, in which the listed performers included one Mansaku and "Mansaku's pupil, Saitō Jūrōbei." According to Mr. Kōno, "Mansaku" was Hōshō Mansaku, of the Hōshō school of Nō. His name appears on a number of occasions in official performances for the shogun's family, but the name of Saitō Jūrōbei is to be found only this once. Even so, the fact that there was a real man of this name, a Nō actor of the Hōshō school, alive around the end of the Bunka era is now certain.

The next question is that of the connection between this man and Awa. Significant in this connection is a document giving details of the stipends of low-ranking persons in the service of the lords of Awa and Awaji. Drawn up in the eighth month of 1792, it was discovered by Mr. Gotō Shōichi, who reported on it in a newspaper in Tokushima, Shikoku (former Awa province), on February 15, 1956. The list of official actors included in this document names, at the bottom of a group of five actors living in Edo, "Saitō Jūrōbei." If this man and the Nō actor already mentioned were one and the same person, then it seems very likely that he was, in fact, in the service of the Lord of Awa.

This does not mean, of course, that one can unhesitatingly identify Sharaku and Saitō Jūrōbei, since one must also take into account—in view of the comparative lateness of the Gesshin version and our ignorance of the theory's provenance—the possibility of Gesshin having been misinformed. Until the discovery of some incontrovertible basic source directly linking the print artist and the Nō actor, we must continue to handle the question with caution.

There are two further sources of information, dating from a period close to the time when Sharaku was active, which must be mentioned here. One of them is the popular novelette (*kibyōshi*), *Shotōzan Tenarai-jō*, written and illustrated by Jippensha Ikku and published in 1796. One of the illustrations to this work shows a large kite with a picture depicting an actor—apparently Ichikawa Ebizō—in the chief role of the kabuki play *Shibaraku*, and inscribed with the characters "Tōshūsai Sharaku." This is probably the earliest occurrence of the name Sharaku we have in the absence of the original of the first version of the *Ukiyo-e Ruikō*. The text of the novelette is entirely facetious, and no account whatsoever is given of the picture; all that one can deduce from it is that Ikku must have had some knowledge of and interest—however faint—in Sharaku, though some scholars attach considerable importance to this evidence. Professor Nakamura Yukihiko of Kyushu University, for instance, considers it possible that Ikku—who was interested in art, who was also a keen kabuki enthusiast, and who, moreover, was engaged around the year 1794 in helping in the production of color prints—fell in with a Nō actor-cum-artist named Sharaku at the premises of the print publisher Tsutaya Jūzaburō. In this he agrees with the theory of Kuramoto Chōji, who in a piece entitled "Fantasy on Sharaku," published in No. 4, Vol. X of *Biography (Denki)* postulated a friendship between the two men.

The second reference to Sharaku is a kind of chart entitled *Yamato-e-shi no Nazukushi* ("A Survey of Yamato-e Artists"), showing schools of ukiyo-e painters past and present in graphic form, schools and artists being represented by islands, promontories, etc., floating in the sea. It was included in another *kibyōshi* entitled *Kusa-zōshi Kojitsuke Nendaiki*, written and illustrated by Shikitei Samba and published in 1802. In this chart, Sharaku is shown as an isolated island, in the same way as Utamaro and Hokusai. That a man with a fondness for historical accuracy such as Samba should have accorded Sharaku such treatment suggests that even in his time Sharaku was already more or less well known as an artist.

There is a large amount of work on Sharaku done since the Meiji Restoration of which mention might be made here. It includes the theory that Sharaku's real name was Shundō Jizaemon, and the discovery of a tomb supposed to be his, both the result of work by the late Dr. Torii Ryūzō; studies which were published in Tokushima newspapers in reply to Dr. Torii's theories; further investigations by Dr. Torii; the research done by the late Nakada Katsunosuke on the basis of these studies; and, more recently, the studies made on the spot in Tokushima City by Yoshida Teruji. Yet the biographical data uncovered by so much labor on the part of so many scholars has been almost negligible.

The result has been to encourage all kinds of theories based on imagination rather than established fact. Thus Sharaku has been identified variously with the painters Tani Bunchō and Maruyama Ōkyo, with the print artist Katsushika Hokusai, and even with his own publisher, Tsutaya Jūzaburō. Yet none of these theories has found general acceptance, nor has a more recent identification of Sharaku with the lacquerware artist Iizuka Tōyō.

In short, Sharaku's life remains for us a few shadows without substance. His works, on the other hand—more than one hundred and fifty of them— are with us, a solid, incontrovertible reality. At the very least, we can focus our attention on those works, and through them learn what we may of his activities and the artistry that inspired him.

The Background

Research has established more or less authoritatively that the portraits of actors by Sharaku which survive today were all produced around the years 1794–5. A preliminary to understanding Sharaku's art, therefore, is to make a brief survey of the state of the ukiyo-e and kabuki at this period.

The Kansei era, along with the immediately preceding Temmei era (1781–88), constituted a kind of golden age for the ukiyo-e, and indeed for Edo culture as a whole. The notorious corruption and laxity of government under Tanuma Okitsugu, minister of the shogunate during the Temmei era had had, paradoxically enough, the effect of stimulating the arts and literature in Edo, which was a predominantly consumer city. The culture of Kyoto and Osaka flowed into the city, and was assimilated to produce the characteristic cultural flowering of the age. Before long, Tanuma came to grief and was succeeded by Matsudaira Sadanobu, who carried out the Kansei reforms, which in turn gave a new flavor to the culture inherited from the preceding era. Whereas the culture of the Temmei era, though promoted chiefly by the merchant class, had reflected the mentality of those members of the samurai class who had been assimilated into the merchant class and of the more leisured, intellectual members of the merchant class itself, the culture of the Kansei era took greater account of the genuine tastes of the merchants themselves, as well as benefiting from a progressive refinement of techniques. Under the sobering influence of the reforms, even the frivolous novelettes of the day began to show a greater respect for reason and order, and the humorous and satirical verse known as *kyōka* manifested an increasing concern with poetic technique as opposed to mere facetiousness. In the field of drama, the appearance in Edo of the Osakan playwright Namiki Gohei checked some of the wilder absurdities of kabuki dramaturgy. And with the ukiyo-e, there was an unmistakable trend toward a greater realism, though not at the expense of poetic atmosphere.

In its first origins, the actor-picture had few artistic pretensions, consisting mostly of the attempts made by artists of the Torii school—a school of painters working exclusively for the theater—to convey a generalized idea of the atmosphere of the kabuki and particular actors. However, with increasing cultural sophistication, and the rise of the realistic outlook in particular, the lifelike portrayal of individual actors' faces as seen in the work of Ippitsusai Buncho and Katsukawa Shunsho, two artists of the Meiwa (1764–1771) and An'ei (1772–1781) eras, came to usurp the place hitherto held by the work of the Torii school. The emphasis on likeness they initiated was to be an indispensable feature of the actor-picture ever after. The actor-pictures of Kiyonaga, the man generally considered to have restored the Torii school's flagging fortunes, show clear signs of an effort to get away from the traditional manner of his school and to produce portraits which were true to life yet not simply imitations of the work of the Katsukawa school. It was only natural, perhaps, that this new striving for facial realism should lead to a concentration on the half-length portrait (okubi-e), and eventually on the face alone (ogao-e). Such portraits enjoyed an enormous vogue, chiefly under the aegis of the Katsukawa school, from the first half of the Kansei era on.

Such were the times that produced Sharaku's own actor-portraits. One thing that should be noted here, however, is that the kabuki at this period was by no means at its most flourishing. The three troupes which were officially licensed to give performances in Edo—the Nakamura-za at Sakai-cho, the Ichimura-za at Fukiya-cho and the Morita-za at Kobiki-cho—were obliged during the middle years of the Kansei era to suspend performances on account of bad business, and to carry on semi-official business under the names of Miyako-za, Kiri-za, and Kawarazaki-za respectively. The trouble, however, did not lie in any decline in the technique or popularity of the actors themselves. The direct cause lay, rather, in financial difficulties due to the swelling costs involved in running the theater as a result of the public demand for extravagant productions. The interest and adulation accorded the actor as such by the average layman seems to have been as intense as ever, nor does it seem that either production of pictures of actors by the professional painter or the output of the print publishing houses diminished in comparison with the preceding age. Indeed, where refinement of technique and richness of artistic content were concerned, the percentage of fine works would seem to have been particularly great in the Kansei era.

Such were the circumstances under which the prints of Sharaku put in their appearance. As to what prompted them or by what process they came into being, however, we are lamentably and totally ignorant. We have no idea, even, of whether they were made for sale or intended for free distribution. The extravagance of using mica dust; the deliberate choice of comparatively low-ranking actors along with their more famous colleagues as subjects for half-length portraits; and the fact that all Sharaku's prints were published by the firm of Tsutaya Jūzaburō—such things would suggest an order from a particular sponsor for prints to be distributed for a particular purpose. However, since no more can be said on this subject without further studies, let us leave it and turn immediately to an analysis and classification of the works of Sharaku that survive with us today.

THE SURVIVING WORKS

The efforts of the various scholars already mentioned have gradually brought to light further examples of Sharaku's work, and the grand total at the present moment, as given in Yoshida Teruji's *Sharaku* (1957) stands at 159 prints—142 polychrome prints and 17 preliminary sketches *(han-shita-e)*. In fact, Professor Yoshida has since eliminated one work from the list of polychromes, a collection of tiny figures suggesting a sheet intended for children; the seal which says "Sharaku" and the form of the publisher's mark incline me to agree that it is not genuine.

As to the names of the roles depicted in the remaining 141 works, there have been minor disagreements among various authorities, but thanks to the studies of Henderson and Ledoux, the broad outlines have now been for the most part agreed upon, while further detailed investigation by Professor Yoshida would seem to have pinpointed the actors concerned as those who appeared in performances from the kabuki season in the fifth month of 1794 to the New Year season of 1795. The present author is not qualified to challenge the results of such painstaking studies, but I believe that there is still room for inquiry into the particular roles depicted. Moreover, not all the basic evidence—the *ehon banzuke*, the *yakuwari (mon) banzuke* and other types of program—has yet been brought to light, which means that there is probably room for further study of the grouping of those color prints that were intended as sets.

I happened recently to come across a number of *ehon banzuke* for the years 1794–5, among them some which seem not to have been taken into account in previous works on Sharaku. Although in the main they in no way upset—tending, if anything, to confirm—the accepted theories concerning the roles depicted, I feel that one can glean from them at least some additional information, and that they help correct a number of minor slips on the part of earlier scholars. I have embodied the results of my use of these new materials in my ordering of and notes on the plates, so I will proceed here to a study of the works as such.

The majority of Sharaku's polychrome prints are pictures of actors, with a few pictures of sumo wrestlers and warrior heroes. The work of Henderson and Ledoux, supplemented by that of Yoshida Teruji and other Japanese scholars, has divided Sharaku's surviving work into the following groups, arranged in chronological order, and this arrangement is generally accepted nowadays.

1. Twenty-eight prints inspired by plays performed by the three kabuki troupes during the fifth month of the 1794 season. All are half-length portraits, *ōban* size (38.2 × 23 cm.), with mica-dust backgrounds. The specific plays with which they deal are:

   Hana-ayame Bunroku Soga, performed by the Miyako-za (11 prints).
   Kataki-uchi Noriyai-banashi, performed by the Kiri-za (7 prints).
   Koi Nyōbō Somewake Tazuna and *Yoshitsune Sembon-zakura*, performed by the Kawarazaki-za (ten prints).

2. Thirty-eight prints inspired by plays put on in the seventh and eighth months of the same year. Of these, eight are *ōban* size with mica-dust backgrounds, while 30 are *hosoban* size (33 × 14.3 cm.). All are full-length portraits. The names of the plays are:

   Keisei Sambon Karakasa, performed in the seventh month by the Miyako-za (17 prints, 4 *ōban* size and 13 *hosoban*).
   Nihon-matsu Michinoku Sodachi and the *Katsura-gawa Tsuki no Omoide*, performed in the seventh month by the Kawarazaki-za (10 prints, 2 *ōban* and 8 *hosoban*).
   Shinrei Yaguchi no Watashi and *Yomo no Nishiki Kokyō no Tabiji*, performed in the eighth month by the Kiri-za (11 prints, 2 *ōban* and 9 *hosoban*).

3. Sixty-one prints depicting plays performed during the kabuki season in the eleventh month of the same year, and wrestlers who participated in the sumo tournament held in the same month. Three are *ōban* size, 13 *aiban* (34.5 × 22.6 cm.), and 45 *hosoban*. Three of the *aiban* prints are half-length portraits, the rest are full-length. They break down as follows:

   Uruou-toshi Meika no Homare, performed by the Miyako-za (18 prints, 2 *aiban* and 16 *hosoban*).
   Hana no Miyako Kuruwa no Nawabari, performed by the Miyako-za in the intercalary eleventh month (2 *aiban* prints).
   Otoko-yama O-Edo no Ishizue, performed by the Kiri-za (21 prints, 4 *aiban* and 17 *hosoban*).
   Matsuwa Misao Onna Kusunoki, performed by the Kawarazaki-za (14 prints, 2 *aiban* and 12 *hosoban*).
   Two *aiban* prints in memory of the actor Ichikawa Monnosuke.
   Four sumo-prints, one *aiban* and three *ōban* forming a triptych.

4. Fourteen prints inspired by plays performed during the New Year season,

1795, together with sumo- and warrior-pictures. They consist of one *ōban*, three *aiban*, and ten *hosoban* prints, and all are full-length portraits. Details are as follows:

Nido no Kake Katsuiro Soga, performed by the Kiri-za (3 *hosoban* prints).

Edo Sunago Kichirei Soga and *Godairiki Koi no Fujime,* performed by the Miyako-za (7 *hosoban* prints).

One *ōban* sumo-picture, two *aiban* warrior-pictures, one other *aiban* picture.

These four main groups illustrate with extraordinary accuracy the changes and development that occurred in Sharaku's art. All the prints in the first group are *ōban* size and employ mica-dust backgrounds; moreover, they are all half-length portraits and maintain a high artistic standard. In the second group there are a few *ōban* prints using mica-dust, but the majority are *hosoban* prints with backgrounds in a single, flat color. The *ōban* prints, with the exception of one full-length portrait of a single actor, are all full-length portraits of pairs of actors; they are fine works with a taut, powerful beauty. The *hosoban* prints, which are all full-length portraits of single actors, are of a similarly high quality and include some sets which betray an astonishing skill in arrangement of the figures. The signature in these first two groups, incidentally, is invariably "Tōshūsai Sharaku," with beneath it the official censor's seal and the Mt. Fuji-with-ivy-leaf trademark of the publisher, Tsutaya Jūzaburō.

In the third group there are over a dozen *aiban* prints—the first time this size puts in its appearance—and the actor-pictures among them are all half-length portraits set against flat-yellow backgrounds. All the *hosoban* prints, the most numerous group, show full-length, single figures, but there is a marked increase in the number of them which have backgrounds intended to link together a set of prints. In this group, however, there is a sudden decline in artistic distinction and power. Another feature of the prints of this period is that only six are signed Tōshūsai Sharaku, the rest having a simple Sharaku. In the same period, the actor-pictures are joined by one *ōban* triptych and one *aiban* print showing sumo wrestlers. The fourth group consists of a large number of *hosoban* actor-pictures, together with one *ōban* sumo-print and a few *aiban* prints of warriors and other subjects. Artistically speaking, this group is the most inferior.

The thing that strikes one here is that Sharaku's art seems to have progressed in a reverse direction from the normal. The usual course followed by ukiyo-e artists took them from a comprehensive treatment of the whole subject together with its background, to a full-length treatment of isolated figures without a background, and thence to the half-length figure; from the small print to the large print; and from technical simplicity to technical complexity. Sharaku traveled in precisely the opposite direction. We have seen above how he turned from the half-length to the full-length figure, from the *ōban* to the *hosoban*. Where printing techniques were concerned, the simplification did not merely involve giving up mica-dust backgrounds in favor of flat colors, but also, in the third and fourth groups, the abandoning of other elaborate and troublesome printing techniques as well. Whether Sharaku was beset by some extraordinarily rapid decline in his physical and mental powers, or whether he compromised his art on account of public indifference or the importunings of his publisher, it is difficult to say. One can only, as one considers the artistic value of each period, note the change and acknowledge, with wonder, what is unmistakable.

THE ART OF SHARAKU

As we have just seen, Sharaku's art reached its zenith during production of the first two groups of prints listed above. Both groups—the first through the half-length, the second through the full-length portrait—are overwhelmingly powerful in their portrayal of character. In the first group, the accuracy and economy with which the line captures only what is essential, dispensing with all unnecessary detail; the way in which eyes, mouth, and hands are used to suggest the spirit within; and in particular the consummate skill with which a fragment of gesture is made to suggest the whole unseen figure are all worthy of the highest admiration. Yet most astonishing of all is the intense and unrelenting artistry which Sharaku reveals in his treatment of facial features—the way in which the angle of the eyes, the line of the nose, the curve of the lips—whose lines at first glance appear to be freakishly distorted—prove on closer inspection to constitute what one might describe as quintessential units of form which are produced by paring away everything but the absolutely indispensable, then subtly arranged so as to give, not merely a facial likeness of the actor being portrayed, but hints of his stature as an actor and the quality of his art, and even a rough idea of his age. Here, Sharaku stands alone; in such respects the ukiyo-e had never seen his like, nor was it to see it again.

The backgrounds of dark-gray mica dust which he uses in these prints are immensely effective in throwing the face into prominence, almost as though it were viewed in a mirror. Things such as this make one realize that Sharaku also had a considerable understanding of the purely technical aspects of printmaking. Not only in his backgrounds, but in his use of color as well, he tried various means to suggest texture and mass as far as possible by flat-color surfaces, saving the brighter colors for very sparing application at crucial points, thus achieving an even greater effect than if they had been used lavishly. The use of flat-color surfaces to suggest mass was a feature of the polychrome print as a whole at that time, but the skill with which the method is used is particularly great in Sharaku's work.

The second group of works, the full-length portraits, maintains the same artistic qualities as the first. Particularly fine are the group of *ōban* prints each showing two figures against a white mica-dust background; in these, the artistic interest lies in the subtle interplay between the two figures, and the tug and balance of personalities holds the same fascination as a confrontation between two ideally matched wrestlers. The *hosoban* prints in the same group show only one standing figure in each work, yet despite the confined nature of the medium, their spiritual power is undiminished. These *hosoban* prints were intended to form sets, and when one places what seem to be related prints alongside each other they do, indeed, seem to acquire a still more vigorous life of their own. One is free, of course, to enjoy them as one pleases, whether separately or in contrast with each other, but in some cases the evidence of the *banzuke* makes it possible to arrange surviving *hosoban* prints in what seems to be the correct order, so that one can get some idea of what Sharaku really intended.

The subtle, organic relationship between these works, which gives aesthetic pleasure even where there is no linking background—or rather, precisely because there is no background—is suddenly dissipated in the works of the third group, where one has a sense that the half-hearted attempt at a background somehow cramps the conversation between the figures it is intended to relate. The indefinable massiveness of scale once observable in Sharaku's work has here shrunk and dwindled. The inner spirituality has vanished, to be replaced by a blatant preoccupation with the depiction of external features and bizarre postures. The *aiban* half-length portraits retain some of the old spiritual quality, but still more apparent is a striving after the merely decorative. This decline becomes even more apparent in the fourth group of works. There is a coarsening of the line, and a distressing desiccation of feeling. The appearance in the third and fourth groups of sumo-pictures and warrior-pictures may indicate that Sharaku himself sensed the deterioration in his art, and tried a change of subject as a way out of the impasse. But the works in question, though nothing by Sharaku could ever be quite devoid of interest, exude an indefinable air of desolation, as of an artist about to lay aside his brush forever. A Japanese poet once wrote of the chill that touched his spine whenever he came up against the loneliness in Sharaku's work. Doubtless he had in mind the work of Sharaku's prime; yet it was in the artist's last work that the loneliness the poet sensed was really to come to the fore, brought out by the numbness that held his art in its clutches.

Such, in brief, were the transitions through which Sharaku's art passed.

The question remains of his artistic pedigree—of the sources from which his characteristic composition and style derived. Nakada Katsunosuke rates the influence of Kiyonaga high, and also cites the inspiration derived from Shunkō and Shun'ei. Yoshida Teruji, in an unusual argument, stresses the influence of Shunshō and Kiyonaga, especially the latter. It is true that things such as the extraordinary elongation of the bodies, or the power and grace of the curving parallel layers of cloth at the wide openings of the sleeves, echo the Kiyonaga style faithfully. But I myself am more inclined to see, in the virility and resilience of Sharaku's line, a derivation from painting, as opposed to the print, and at first would have suggested the Kanō school as a possible source. However, having since had the resemblance to the brushwork of the Soga school pointed out to me, I am now disposed to accept the same view myself.

Where the supposed influence of Shunshō is concerned, I feel more inclined to agree than in the case of Kiyonaga, since in the postures of Sharaku's actors one senses something that, though in the general manner of the Kansei era, also reminds one indefinably of the style of the preceding Temmei era, when Shunshō reigned supreme. Moreover, there are certain Sharaku works which resemble works of Shunshō in their actual composition. For all the individuality of Sharaku's art, I feel it is unlikely that he would have relied entirely on practice in sketching from life without any reference whatsoever to the work of his predecessors. There are other indications, moreover, that this was indeed not so. For example, the portraits of Yamashita Kinsaku to be found among groups (3) and (4) mentioned above resemble those found in *Yakusha Monoiwai*, a picture book of actors by Ryūkōsai Jokei of Osaka, and Ryūkōsai's *Ehon Niwatazumi* also seems to afford certain resemblances. It would be rash immediately to assume some connection between the two men, but the resemblances suggest a possibly fruitful line of investigation.

Preoccupied with Sharaku's polychrome prints, I have left little space for discussion of his painting. Eight works which seem to be preliminary designs for actor-prints—most of such designs have been lost—together with nine preliminary designs for prints of sumo wrestlers have generally been considered to be the work of Sharaku. The latter exist now only in photograph form, the originals having been lost in the Great Earthquake of 1923, and even the former are available only as photographs in Japan, the originals having gone abroad. However, so far as I can judge from such evidence, the sumo-pictures are somewhat inferior to the actor-pictures. The latter are considered not to represent scenes from any particular kabuki play, but to be arbitrary compositions based on *ehon banzuke*.

Recently, in examining these pictures analytically, I have come across one or two rather perplexing stylistic features. Only one of the actor-pictures has Sharaku's signature, and Professor Nakada judged, from having seen the photograph, that this signature had been pasted on afterwards. In fact, according to a report made by Mr. Packard, after a recent trip abroad during which he had a chance to inspect the originals, the section bearing the signature had been cut out, a new piece of paper pasted on from the back, then the whole back of the print covered with a new piece of paper. It seems probable then that the signature was a later addition by other hands. Again, where the remaining seven pictures are concerned, there are a number of sections of the figures which resemble corresponding sections in Sharaku's prints. Is one, then, to come to the rather disappointing conclusion that even a man as noted for his originality as Sharaku could sometimes resort to making compositions simply by arranging ready-made parts—as was the practice among other Japanese artists in days gone by?

There are other troubling features about these pictures. All seven of them show joins down their centers. Three of them, too, have borders round all four sides, which may mean that they were designed for a picture book or an album. I am not rash enough to attempt any logical explanation of all these questions without a far more thorough study of the original works; I would merely suggest, for those interested, that there are matters here that require looking into. Mr. Packard, apparently, is inclined to the view that the materials in question are spurious. Either way, here again one is left with the feeling that whatever path of investigation one chooses to follow with Sharaku, one comes across nothing but mysteries.

A word, finally, about the influence of Sharaku on other artists. For all the talk of his unpopularity in the *Ukiyo-e Ruikō*, the size of his output in relation to the short period in which he worked makes it seem likely that he had a certain following. Other factors too—the subsequent appearance of artists such as Kabukidō Enkyō and Utagawa Kunimasa, whose work bears certain resemblances to his, and the resemblance to Sharaku's works in the composition of pictures painted on round fans depicted in pictures of celebrated beauties done by Chōki and Eiri—tend to confirm this, and suggest that his work was current in a definite, if limited, sphere of society. More than once it has occurred to me to wonder just what emotions Sharaku would feel if, from his vantage point in the other world, he could witness the popularity of his works today—how they appear on calendars, on postage stamps, and even in commercial trademarks. And I like to think of him watching and evaluating, with the same sardonic detachment as ever, the ways in which his work is put to use.

Notes to the Plates

The prints reproduced in the following pages are arranged in the order of performance of the plays which they illustrate. Where plays were performed by different troupes in the same month, the prints are grouped by theater. The names of the plays and roles are taken from the various *banzuke*.

Plates 2–12 are based on *Hana-ayame Bunroku Soga*. The libretto does not survive, but the *ehon banzuke* and *yakuwari banzuke* show it to have been a complex tale of revenge taken by three sons for the murder of their father. The oldest son is himself killed by the enemy, and it is only twenty years later that the remaining brothers finally redeem the family honor.

Plates 13–19 are based on the play *Kataki-uchi Noriyai-banashi*. The play is a weaving together of two other works, *Kataki-uchi Ganryū-jima* and *Go Taiheiki Shiraishi-banashi;* the roles Sharaku depicts all come from the *Shiraishi-banashi* part or from a dance number entitled *Hana Shōbu Omoi no Kanzashi* which was performed at the same time. The play is the story of the revenge taken by two sisters, Miyagino and Shinobu, for their father Matsushita Mikinoshin, who has been murdered by Shiga Daishichi.

Plates 20–27, and 80 are based on *Koi Nyōbō Somewake Tazuna*, a tale of intrigue in great families, and Plate 28 on two scenes from *Yoshitsune Sembon-zakura*, which was performed on the same program. The latter, one of the most famous of puppet drama and kabuki plays, is based on the story of the celebrated twelfth-century hero Minamoto no Yoshitsune.

Plates 29–40 are based on the play *Keisei Sambon Karakasa*. The libretto has not survived. An *ehon banzuke*, however, shows that the plot deals with a well-known story of a power struggle within a noble family, and with the opposition between the villain, Fuwa no Banzaemon, and the hero, Nagoya Sanza. The story has typical kabuki highlights—the plot of Fuwa to make himself head of the family, the flight of the infant lord in the care of a faithful retainer, the encounter of villain and hero in the gay quarters, etc.

Plates 41–47 are based on *Nihon-matsu Michinoku Sodachi* and *Katsura-gawa Tsuki no Omoide*, on the same program. The *ehon banzuke* for the first piece suggests that the plot was a blend of elements from the "Date affair," a famous tale of intrigue and revenge, and the story of the Nihon-matsu vendetta. The latter tells how Tomida Heitarō, with the aid of Saburōbei, a bean-curd vendor, takes revenge on the villain, Kawashima Jibugorō, for the murder of his father, Tomida Sukedayū. The second play is based on the popular love story of Ohan and Chōemon, who committed double suicide in the Katsura River.

Plates 48–56 are inspired by two plays performed at the same time, *Shinrei Yaguchi no Watashi* and *Yomo no Nishiki Kokyō no Tabiji*. The plot of the former tells how Nitta Yoshisada, a famous general in the fourteenth century, is killed in a battle with the Ashikaga family, who later became virtual rulers of Japan. His son Yoshioki is also defeated and killed, and his wife Tsukuba Gozen and infant son Tokuju-maru roam the country attended by the faithful retainer Minase Rokurō. Another important figure is the wise retainer Yura Hyōgonosuke, who temporarily sides with the enemy in order to protect Tokuju-maru, and even kills his own son as a substitute for Tokuju-maru. The other play is the well-known story of the tragic love of Chūbei and the courtesan Umegawa.

Plates 57–61 are based on the play *Uruou-toshi Meika no Homare*. Names that appear in the program suggest that the main theme was the complex struggle for the throne between the princes Koretaka and Korehito that occurred in the Heian Period, and that various celebrated poets of that period also put in an appearance.

Plate 62 is based on *Hana no Miyako Kuruwa no Nawabari*. The play was the first written in Edo by the well-known Osaka playwright Namiki Gohei.

Plates 63–72 are drawn from *Otoko-yama O-Edo no Ishizue*. Names of various historical personages such as Abe no Sadatō and Hachiman Tarō occur, but details of the plot are not known.

Plates 73 and 74 are based on *Matsuwa Misao Onna Kusunoki* and *Kagura-zuki Iwai no Iroginu*, a dance number that occurs within it. The play seems to have drawn its plot from the *Taiheiki*, a chronicle in poetic prose of the twelfth-century struggle between the Taira and Minamoto clans.

Plates 75 and 76 show prints made in memory of the actor Ichikawa Monnosuke II, who died in 1794 at the age of fifty-two.

Plates 77 and 78 are based on *Nido no Kake Katsuiro Soga*. It was customary for all theaters to present a piece dealing with the Soga vendetta at the New Year, and though there were variations, they usually included the scene showing the confrontation between the Soga brothers and their enemy, Kudō.

Plate 79 is an example of Sharaku's sumo-pictures.

32

東洲斎 写楽画

1. *The Director of the Miyako-za Reading a Prologue* ◈ *ōban* ◈ mica-dust background ◈ The Metropolitan Museum of Art, Whittelsey Fund, 1949 ◈ The writing on the paper which the director holds in his hands (it is not visible in this copy of the print) says, "We shall now submit for your approval a second series of hitherto unpublished portraits," which has been interpreted as an announcement that Sharaku was about to switch from his series of half-length portraits to his full-length series. The portrayal of the face is masterly, and the colors of the clothing complement the white mica dust of the background.

33

2. *Segawa Kikunojō III as Oshizu, wife of Tanabe Bunzō* ◆ *ōban* ◆ mica-dust background ◆ Hiraki Shinji collection ◆ Oshizu joins her husband in helping the hero take revenge on his enemy. Kikunojō was celebrated as the most beautiful *onnagata* (female impersonator) of his day, and this print captures the grace and femininity of his acting, an effect which is heightened by the beautiful coloring. The surprising smallness of the hand tucked inside the obi probably represents a conscious deformation intended to suggest the character's smallness and helplessness. The print is a masterpiece to be numbered among the best of Sharaku's half-length portraits of *onnagata*.

34

3. *Segawa Tomisaburō II as Yadorigi, wife of Ōgishi Kurando, and Nakamura Manyo as Koshimoto Wakakusa* ◆ *ōban* ◆ mica-dust background ◆ Nomura Shigeyuki collection ◆ The interest of this print, of course, is the contrast between the long, skinny face of Tomisaburō, with its prominent jawline, and Manyo's round, plump face. The excessive downward droop of Manyo's hands in contrast with the graceful upward curve of Tomisaburō's does some violence to nature, but one can only marvel at the extraordinary perception with which Sharaku uses this to sum up the whole style of Manyo's performance.

35

4. *Segawa Tomisaburō II as Yadorigi, wife of Ōgishi Kurando* ◆ *ōban* ◆ mica-dust background ◆ Tokyo National Museum ◆ Tomisaburō, a pupil of Segawa Kikunojō III, was often called by his nicknames of "Hateful Tomi" and "Nasty Tomi"—presumably because of a certain angularity in his personal appearance. This would seem to be borne out by the pronounced jawline seen beneath the ear in this print. The effect is sardonic yet precise.

5. *Sanogawa Ichimatsu III as Onayo Hakujin of Gion, and Ichikawa Tomiemon as Kanisaka Tōma* ◆ *ōban* ◆ mica-dust background ◆ The Art Institute of Chicago, Buckingham Collection of Japanese Prints ◆ In the illustrated program, Ichimatsu is listed as playing Onayo for some two months, but nothing definite is known of the part the character plays in the drama. The name of Tomiemon's role has always been thought to be "Tōta," but both the *ehon banzuke* and the *yakuwari banzuke* have "Tōma," the former even having the name written phonetically in one place. Tōma is one of the villains of the piece. In strong contrast to Ichimatsu's narrow, aristocratic face with its arched eyebrows, Tomiemon's broad, flat face conveys the vulgar, essentially minor character of the role.

37

6. *Bandō Mitsugorō II as Ishii Genzō* ◆ *ōban* ◆ mica-dust background ◆ Boston Museum of Fine Arts, Spaulding Collection ◆ This picture has always been believed to represent the scene where Ishii attacks Mizuemon. The *ehon banzuke*, however, shows this to be an error; it is, in fact, the scene where, together with his wife Chizuka, he meets death at the hands of the very enemy he seeks to kill. The pose, with sword held diagonally across his body, is imbued with power and movement and the embossed pattern on the white undergarment is strikingly effective.

7. *Sakata Hangorō III as Fujikawa Mizu-emon* ◈ *ōban* ◈ mica-dust background ◈ The Art Institute of Chicago, Buckingham Collection of Japanese Prints ◈ The print captures perfectly the atmosphere of extreme wickedness surrounding the principal villain of the piece, a man who will stop at nothing, tenance, looming weird and aggressive out of the somber background, is particularly fine, and the work ranks among Sharaku's very finest.

8. *Arashi Ryūzō as Ishibe Kinkichi the money-lender* ◆ *ōban* ◆ mica-dust background ◆ Yamamoto Kiyoo collection ◆ According to the *ehon banzuke*, this character appears in the latter half of the play. He is apparently a Shy-lock-type moneylender who comes to press Tanabe Bunzō for repayment just when the lat-ter is going through his leanest period. The un-usual cast of countenance, with the lips com-pressed into one straight line, is precisely what one would expect in such a part. The left sleeve, partly rolled back as though for action of some kind, is especially effective.

40

9. *Sanogawa Ichimatsu III as Onayo Hakujin of Gion* ◆ *ōban* ◆ mica-dust background ◆ Tokyo National Museum ◆ Ichimatsu at first played female roles, but later changed his name to Ichikawa Aragorō and switched to male roles, a fact which suggests that there was something essentially stiff and unfeminine about him. This print, in fact, clearly shows him to have been a rather grim *onnagata*, not especially endowed with good looks. The pattern on the kimono later came to be popularly known as "Ichimatsu," after the actor.

10. *Ōtani Tokuji as the servant Sodesuke* ◆
ōban ◆ mica-dust background ◆ The Art
Institute of Chicago, Buckingham Collection
of Japanese Prints ◆ A servant of one of the
good characters, Sodesuke is seen in the *ehon
banzuke* informing Ishii Hyōe's eldest son
Genzō of his father's violent death and engaged in a fight with the villains. This particular print would seem to be based on the
scene of the fight, since he is shown drawing
his sword. Tokuji was the leading actor for
comic parts at the time, and even here there
is something faintly humorous about the
face, hands, and the whole posture of the
body. In this print the signature is tucked
away in the bottom right-hand corner––or
in some versions the upper left-hand corner.

11. *Sawamura Sōjūrō III as Ōgishi Kurando* ◆ *ōban* ◆ mica-dust background ◆ Yamamoto Kiyoo collection ◆ The leading "good" character in the play, his informal, relaxed pose suggests that he is seen here in the scene in the Gion gay quarters. The hand, fan, and face, which constitute a kind of foreground, middle distance and background respectively, give the composition a natural sense of perspective, while the way in which the actor's body occupies most of the lower half of the picture gives the print a sense of unhurried stability. The actor portrayed was very popular in his day, noted for his fine bearing and good looks. A big man, he played in both historical and contemporary dramas, and was skilled at both romantic and character parts. The print captures all these qualities.

43

12. *Ichikawa Yaozō III as Tanabe Bunzō* ◆ *ōban*
◆ mica-dust background ◆ Boston Museum of
Fine Arts, Spaulding Collection ◆ This particular character, it has often been claimed, is one of
the people killed by Fujikawa Mizuemon, the
villain of the play, but this is a mistake. The illustrated program shows that he runs to the scene
of the attack on Ishii Genzō and his wife, and is
himself wounded on the thigh by Mizuemon,

becoming a cripple as a result. After many hard-
ships, he completely recovers and joins Ishii's son
in revenging his murdered father. This print apparently shows him dressed as a masterless samurai during the period when he has fallen on hard
times, and the mournful expression and sober
costume skillfully suggest the reduced circumstances in which he finds himself. The curves of
the pattern on the kimono create an effect of mass.

13. *Matsumoto Yonesaburō as Shinobu, posing
as Kewaizaka no Shōshō* ◆ *ōban* ◆ mica-dust
background ◆ Boston Museum of Fine Arts,
Bigelow Collection ◆ The character depicted
here, one of the two sisters whose father is
murdered, has become a courtesan in order
to obtain revenge on the assassin. In its treatment of the subject, this is one of the mildest
of all Sharaku's portraits of *onnagata*, and the
coloring too is particularly beautiful. The
hand protruding from the kimono is perhaps
unnaturally small, but this is probably a deliberate deformation aimed at suggesting the
character's delicacy and charm.

14. *Onoe Matsusuke as Matsushita Mikinoshin* ◆
ōban ◆ mica-dust background ◆ C.H. Mitchell collection ◆ Matsushita is the man who is
murdered by the Shiga Daishichi of the following print. Matsusuke later changed his name to
Shōroku and specialized in the "vengeful
ghost" type of role, which suggests that his
acting had some essentially gloomy quality

about it. In this print, the hair growing on the
head where it should be shaven, the shadows
around the eyes, the untidy sideburns and top-
knot, and the somber choice of colors not only
suggest the wretched life the character is leading but also convey this inherent quality in
Matsusuke's art.

46

15. *Ichikawa Komazō II as Shiga Daishichi* ◆ *ōban* ◆ mica-dust background ◆ Takahashi Seiichirō collection ◆ The print is believed to show Daishichi, the villain of the piece and also the principal role, in the scene where he kills Matsushita. Komazō later succeeded to the name of Matsumoto Kōshirō V, and was popularly known as "Beaky Kōshirō." As this suggests, he had a characteristic, aquiline profile. In his younger days, he specialized in playing the young man of rank who through special circumstances was forced to go about in humble guise, but he later turned to playing villains. This print shows the blend of masculine appeal and cruelty that one expects from such an actor. The face is thrown into relief by the unrelieved somberness of the background.

47

16. *Nakajima Wadaemon as Bōdara Chō-zaemon and Nakamura Konozō as Gon of the Kanagawaya Boathouse* ◆ *ōban* ◆ mica-dust background ◆ Yamamoto Kiyō collection ◆ In the *ehon banzuke* these two characters are shown very small, and seem to have been relatively unimportant roles, yet the print itself has an artistically satisfying quality that places it among the very best of all Sharaku's twin half-length portraits. Besides the subtle contrast between the skinniness of Wada-emon and the corpulence of Konozō, there is a skillful balance between the contrasting characters of the two actors in such details as the shape and slant of eyes, eyebrows, nose, and mouth.

17. *Nakayama Tomisaburō as Miyagino, the elder of the two daughters left by the murdered Mikinoshin* ◆ *ōban* ◆ mica-dust background ◆ Yamamoto Kiyō collection ◆ The actor's nickname, "Floppy Tomi," was probably inspired by an excessive flexibility in his movements and gestures, a quality which is suggested here in touches such as the outline of the face from the cheek down to the jaw, and the willowiness of the hand and fingers raised to the collar of the kimono. The work is rather unusual among Sharaku's pictures of *onnagata* in its relaxed atmosphere.

49

18. *Matsumoto Kōshirō IV as Gorōbei the Fishmonger of Sanya* ◆ *ōban* ◆ mica-dust background ◆ The Art Institute of Chicago, Buckingham Collection of Japanese Prints ◆ The worthy fishmonger helps the sisters Miyagino and Shinobu seek out their enemy Shiga Daishichi and take revenge on him. Sharaku accurately conveys the good looks and dignity of Kōshirō, an actor with a fine and character roles. There is remarkable skill in the way the use of line on the clothing is kept to a minimum, both the solidity and the softness of the arm being suggested solely by means of the pattern of stripes left standing out white on flat color.

19. *Morita Kanya as Uguisu no Jirosaku the Palanquin-bearer* ◆ *ōban* ◆ mica-dust background ◆ Tokyo National Museum ◆ Jirosaku is a character in the dance *Hana Shōbu* *Omoi no Kanzashi*, which was inserted into the play proper. The print captures precisely the momentary pose, and even the patterns on the costume seem to be moving rhythmically.

20. *Ōtani Oniji as Edohei the manservant* ◇
ōban ◆ mica-dust background ◆ Tokyo
National Museum ◆ This character con-
spires with the villain, Washizuka Happeiji,
to rob Ippei, a follower of Date no Yosaku.
The whole print—with the strong, angular
face thrust forward, the taut, thin line of the
lips, and the hands spread out as though
itching for action—seems almost about to
leap into violent movement. The one serious
fault, perhaps, is the excessive deformation
of the left hand.

21. *Ichikawa Omezō as Ippei the manservant* ◆ *ōban* ◆ mica-dust background ◆ Nomura Shigeyuki collection ◆ From a scene in which Ippei fights single-handed against a group of ruffians, the print captures with dazzling virtuosity one of the momentary, exaggerated poses so typical of kabuki. The work is known as "the red *juban*," because of the red under-garment which affords such an effective contrast with the black. It is generally said that Omezō was only fourteen at the time, but research using the *banzuke* suggests that he was in fact at least ten years older; even so, the suggestion of youth in the face is remarkable.

22. *Tanimura Torazō as Washizuka Happeiji* ◆ *ōban* ◆ mica-dust background ◆ Hiraki Shinji collection ◆ Younger brother of Washizuka Kandayū, one of the villains of the piece, Happeiji is also involved in his brother's evil dealings. Torazō, who was twenty-six at the time, was small of stature and technically proficient, but lacked presence. Contemporary criticism complained—and this print bears it out—that he was not sinister enough for a villain. Sharaku skillfully captures the nature of this actor, whose forte was his portrayal of cheap, petty villains.

23. *Iwai Kiyotarō as Fujinami, wife of Sagi-saka Sanai, and Bandō Zenji as Ozasa, wife of Washizuka Kandayū* ◆ *ōban* ◆ mica-dust background ◆ Mizuta Mikio collection ◆ The chief interest of this work lies in the contrast between the two women—wives of one of the good characters and one of the villains respectively—and between their differing costumes and makeup. Also in-teresting, however, are the variety of the composition and the avoidance of the more usual facing arrangement of the two figures. An interesting balance is created between the two hands—one left, one right—and the composition is skillfully knitted together by making the two pairs of eyes gaze at the same spot.

55

24. *Ichikawa Monnosuke II as Date no Yosaku* ◆
ōban ◆ mica-dust background ◆ Yamamoto
Kiyoo collection ◆ The *ehon banzuke* suggests
that this is the scene where Yosaku is expelled
from his master's house. The pose and the
general bearing are just what one would expect
of a popular actor skilled at romantic parts. In
this print Sharaku shows a sensitivity and a
power of expression of a different type from
that evident in his more powerful, exaggerated
works.

56

25. *Iwai Hanshirō IV as Shigenoi, a wet nurse* ❖ *ōban* ❖ mica–dust background ❖ Nakajima Shin'ichirō collection ❖ Shigenoi is one of the leading female roles of the play. Known popularly as "Mumpsy Hanshirō" on account of his plump, round face, this actor had a brilliant style of acting and a powerful charm which made him, along with Segawa Kikunojō, one of the two most famous *onnagata* of his day. Sharaku's use of warm colors helps bring out this special quality of the subject.

26. *Bandō Hikosaburō III as Sagisaka Sanai* ◆ *ōban* ◆ mica-dust background ◆ C. H. Mitchell collection ◆ Sagisaka is a virtuous character, majordomo for the Yurugi family in the province of Tamba, who gives shelter to Date no Yosaku and helps reinstate him in his lord's service. The role must have been ideal for Hikosaburō, who was noted for his dignified bearing. The *ehon banzuke* suggests that this is the scene in which Sagisaka gives Yosaku advice on how to recover his fortunes. The simplicity of the coloring is offset by the three-dimensional effect created by the skillful placing of the lantern before the left shoulder and the shawl which has fallen behind the right shoulder.

58

27. *Osagawa Tsuneyo II* ◆ ōban ◆ mica-dust background ◆ Takahashi Seiichirō collection ◆ The costume in this print fits neither Osan, daughter of Ippei in the play *Koi-nyōbō Some-wake Tazuna*, nor Shizuka Gozen in *Yoshitsune Sembon-zakura*, both roles which Tsuneyo played on this occasion. None of the surviving *banzuke* names any other role he played, nor has any satisfactory theory yet emerged. Tsuneyo had a solid command of technique and was a master at woeful scenes, but lacked obvious brilliance and charm, his art being described in a contemporary account as "sixty percent fruit and only forty percent flower." The print captures this quality admirably.

59

28. *Bandō Zenji as Oni Sadobō and Sawamura Yodogorō II as Kawatsura Hōgen* ◆
ōban ◆ mica-dust background ◆ Tokyo
National Museum ◆ These are two characters who appear in *Yoshitsune Sembonzaku-
ra*. The taller figure is Kawatsura Hōgen, a
good character who gives shelter to Yoshitsune while he is in flight from his brother,
who seeks to have him killed. The figure
with the shaven head is Oni Sadobō, an evil
priest who is interested in Yoshitsune's down-
fall. The contrast of good and evil is a fa-
vorite technique of Sharaku; especially interesting here is the way the fingers spread
wide—one clenched, the other with fingers
spread wide—are used to give the picture
extra life.

60

29. *Ōtani Hiroji III as the manservant Tosa no Matahei* ◆ *hosoban* ◆ Boston Museum of Fine Arts, Bigelow Collection

30. *Arashi Ryūzō as the manservant Ukiyo Matahei* ◆ *hosoban* ◆ Mizuta Mikio collection

These two prints have been inferred, because of their composition, to form part of a set, and the *ehon banzuke* confirms this. The same *banzuke* also shows that a print of Bandō Mitsugorō as the farmer Fukakusa no Jirosaku should be added on the left to complete the set. The Matahei played by Ryūzō is in the service of the villain Fuwa, while Hiroji's Matahei is a follower of the faithful retainer Nagoya. Ryūzō's stance, feet apart and planted on the ground almost as though they have taken root, has an enormous stability and solidity. Hiroji, on the other hand, has a softly plump body and is striking an old-style pose typical of the early days of kabuki. The rounded lines used in this print carry a suggestion of the Shunshō style of the preceding An'ei and Temmei eras, and afford a clue as to where Sharaku may have found his original inspiration.

61

These three prints show a confrontation between Fuwa and Nagoya in the Shimabara gay quarters of Kyoto. The role of Fuwa is of the type known in Japanese as *iroaku*, a combination of villainy and sex appeal, and the print shown here captures the atmosphere of the role well. In the same way, the print of Sōjūrō as Sanza conveys exactly the romantic, almost slightly effeminate atmosphere of this part. Kikunojō as Katsuraki, standing between the two, has a stage presence befitting the leading *onnagata* of the day, and the way he holds his body, together with details such as the lining showing at the shoulder of the gorgeous outer kimono, convey well the fascination of this type of role. Utagawa Toyokuni portrayed the same three roles—reversing the positions of Fuwa and Nagoya—in a set of prints entitled *Yakusha Butai no Sugata-e.*

31. *Sawamura Sōjūrō III as Nagoya Sanza Motoharu* ◈ *hosobe* ◈ Boston Museum of Fine Arts, Bigelow Collection

. *Segawa Kikunojō III as the courtesan Katsuraki* ◆ *hosoban*
Mizuta Mikio collection

33. *Ichikawa Yaozō III as Fuwa no Banzaemon Shigekatsu* ◆
hosoban ◆ Tokyo National Museum

63

34. *Ōtani Tokuji as Monogusa Tarō* ◆ *hosoban* ◆ Kodaka
Chū collection

35. *Ichikawa Tomiemon as Inokuma Monbei* ◆ *hosoban*
Tokyo National Museum

64

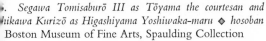

. *Segawa Tomisaburō III as Tōyama the courtesan and ↑hikawa Kurizō as Higashiyama Yoshiwaka-maru* ◆ *hosoban* Boston Museum of Fine Arts, Spaulding Collection

37. *Sakata Hangorō III as Kosodate no Kannonbō* ◆ *hosoban* ◆ The Art Institute of Chicago, Buckingham Collection of Japanese Prints

here has been considerable dispute as to the arrangement ￐ this set of four prints, but pictures in the *ehon banzuke* ￐ow that they should be arranged as seen here, in two airs of two figures each. The courtesan Tōyama has ￐ed with the child Yoshiwaka in her custody following ￐e murder of his father as a result of a plot by the villain ￐wa. These prints apparently show the scene in which ￐e is set upon by the evil priest Kannonbō. The money-￐nder Inokuma Monbei is about to join him when Mono-￐sa Tarō intervenes in defense of Tōyama. The pose of

Hangorō, stiffly upright with arms folded, conveys a wonderful sense of tension, as though a tautly stretched bow ran through the body from the top of the head to the tip of the toes. Equally striking is the pose struck by Tomisaburō, with his body twisted protectively round the child. The figure of Tomiemon, with his hoe still in his hand, successfully suggests the essential lightness of the role, while Tokuji, with his spade held at the ready, is a definitely humorous figure.

65

東洲齋寫樂画

38. *Sakata Hangorō III as Kosodate no Kan-nonbō and Ichikawa Yaozō III as Fuwa no Ban-zaemon* ◆ *ōban* ◆ mica-dust background ◆ The Art Institute of Chicago, Buckingham Collection of Japanese Prints ◆ The threatening pose struck by Hangorō admirably balances the passive posture of Yaozō at his feet, and the picture skillfully suggests two actors whose techniques were perfectly in tune. The tightly organized composition and the beautiful coloring also contribute greatly to the total effect. The composition, however, is very similar to a print by Katsukawa Shunshō showing two actors in another play performed earlier at the Nakamura-za.

66

39. *Ōtani Hiroji III as the manservant Tosa no Matahei and Arashi Ryūzō as the manservant Ukiyo Matahei* ◆ *ōban* ◆ mica-dust background ◆ Tokyo National Museum ◆ This would seem to be a one-print version of the two *hoso-ban* prints in Plates 29 and 30. Both figures— the perspective suggests that they are being viewed from down in the audience—have great solidity and stability, and the poses and expressions convey a most satisfying impression of two actors whose performances are perfectly attuned to each other in every detail.

40. *Sawamura Sōjūrō III as Nagoya Sanza and Segawa Kikunojō III as the courtesan Katsuraki* ◆ *ōban* ◆ mica-dust background ◆ Yamamoto Kiyoo collection ◆ This print shows what is apparently an amorous scene between Sanza and Katsuraki. The composition hinges on a diagonal traversing the print from top-left to bottom-right, the figures themselves being contained within a right-angled triangle which gives a great sense of stability. It is a work of pleasing harmonies and contrasts, the dandified, playboyish figure of Sanza being skillfully offset by the feminine appeal of Katsuraki. The gorgeous colors are given focus in the black of Katsuraki's outer garment, and the whitish mica-dust background gives a sense of richness.

Osagawa Tsuneyo II as Okinu, wife of Chōemon ◆ *hoso-* ◆ Amsterdam Rijksmuseum

42. *Bandō Hikosaburō III as Chōemon the Sash-maker* ◆ *hosoban* ◆ Boston Museum of Fine Arts, Spaulding Collection

Both these prints show characters from *Katsura-gawa Tsuki no Omoide*. In the treatment of the obi and the lines of the body, the print of Okinu conveys the indefinable attraction of the sophisticated matron. Hikosaburō's expression and posture cleverly suggest the nature of the role of Chōemon, which called for stolid worth rather than anything softer and more romantic.

43. *Ichikawa Omezō as Ikazuchi Tsurunosuke the Wrestler and Ōtani Oniji II as Ukiyo Tohei* ◆ *ōban* ◆ mica-dust background ◆ Tokyo National Museum ◆ No details are known about these two roles, but Omezō's hairstyle suggests a wrestler—though it is puzzling that he should carry two swords in the manner of a samurai. The composition is splendidly eccentric. Oniji's pose is interesting, with his kimono tucked up over his buttocks, but more powerful still is the figure of Omezō, kneeling with his right foot thrust forward and his hand on his sword ready to draw it. Another fine touch is the accuracy with which the gaze of both is focused on the same spot.

44. *Bandō Hikosaburō III as Chōemon the Sash-maker and Iwai Hanshirō IV as Ohan of Shinanoya* ◆ *ōban* ◆ mica-dust background ◆ The Art Institute of Chicago, Buckingham Collection of Japanese Prints ◆ This print shows the two lovers Ohan and Chōemon in the famous passage with samisen and voice accompaniment which precedes their double suicide in the *Katsura-gawa Tsuki no Omoide*. Ohan seems to be uttering soft blandishments, while Chōemon stands with arms folded and an appropriate air of masculine sternness.

45. *Ōtani Oniji II as Kawashima Jibugorō* ◆ *hosoban* ◆ Tokyo National Museum ◆ This print shows the point in the play where Jibugorō has just murdered Sukedayū and is about to make off into the night. Oniji's posture alone is enough to put this among the finest of the *hosoban* works, the characteristic bow-like curve, which Sharaku often gives to his figures being particularly fine here. It also seems most likely that the raised right arm is intended to fend off the light of a lantern held up by a character shown in another print which forms a pair with this work.

hikawa Ebizō as Rammyaku no Kichi ◆ hosoban ◆
National Museum ◆ Ebizō also appeared as Saburō-
bean-curd vendor, a similar role, in the other of the
ays on which this group is based, and the dagger he
ere would seem more appropriate to Saburōbei. The
conveys extremely well the majesty and power of
stage presence.

47. *Iwai Kiyotarō as Osode, daughter of Futamiya* ◆ *hosoban* ◆ Hiraki
Shinji collection ◆ Artistically, this ranks among the very best of
the *hosoban* prints. The curves of the pattern on the kimono,
paralleling the curves of the figure, create a pleasing sense of
rhythm and harmony. The way the hand is held and the placing
of the foot emerging from beneath the kimono skillfully suggest
the organic relationship between the two.

73

These three prints are believed to have formed a set, along with one other print—a portrait of Ichikawa Komazō II as Minase Rokurō Munezumi—which came between Tsukuba Gozen and Hyōgonosuke. The costumes and other factors suggest that this represents the scene in which there is a confrontation at the Nitta mansion between Minase (not shown here), who advocates doing battle with the enemy, and Hyōgonosuke, who advocates peace. The figure of Hyōgonosuke in particular seems somehow to suggest the inner struggle of a man who on the surface proposes peace with the enemy yet is secretly aiming to protect the kin of his murdered lord. Minato, on the other hand, who has not realized what her husband is up to, seems to be exuding silent indignation at his pusillanimity.

48. *Nakamura Kumetarō II as Minato, wife of Hyōgonosuke* ◆ *hosoban* ◆ Boston Museum of Fine Arts, Bigelow Collection

9. *Morita Kanya VIII as Yura Hyōgonosuke Nobutada* ◆ *hoso-*
-an ◆ Mizuta Mikio collection

50. *Nakayama Tomisaburō as Tsukuba Gozen, wife of Nitta*
Yoshioki ◆ *hosoban* ◆ The Art Institute of Chicago, Buckingham
Collection of Japanese Prints

These two prints illustrate a scene at the border between two provinces in which Minase Rokurō, disguised as a pilgrim, seeks to pass the barrier with his young lord Tokuju-maru concealed in a basket. Negoto no Chōzō, a bad man, senses something afoot and sets on Rokurō with his fellow ruffians. Here, Rokurō is drawing the sword concealed in his metal pilgrim's staff, the formal beauty of his pose—typical of kabuki sword-fight scenes—contrasting admirably with Kanzō's more active stance.

51. *Nakajima Kanzō as Negoto no Chōzō the Packhorse-driver* ◆ *hoso ban* ◆ Tokyo National Museum

52. *Ichikawa Komazō II as Minase Rokurō Munezumi* ◆ *hosoban*
◆ Tokyo National Museum

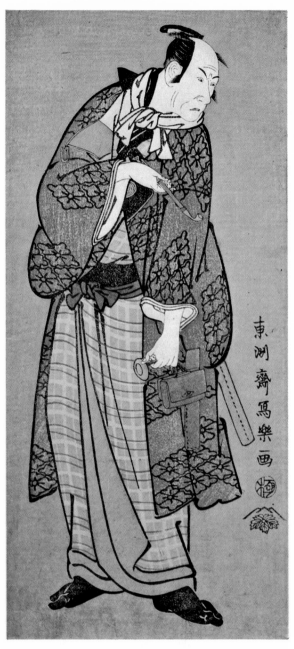

53. *Matsumoto Kōshirō IV as Yamato no Yabo Daijin, in reality Ninokuchimura no Magoemon* ◆ *hosoban* ◆ The Art Institute of Chicago, Buckingham Collection of Japanese Prints

54. *Nakajima Wadaemon as Tambaya Hachiemon* ◆ *hosoban* C. H. Mitchell collection

Both these roles occur in the play *Yomo no Nishiki Kokyō no Tabiji.* Hachiemon is an acquaintance of the Chūbei who occurs in Plate 56. In Chikamatsu's original puppet drama he is portrayed as a man of good sense, often sharp-tongued in defense of Chūbei, but in the kabuki version he is often, as here, apparently shown as more of a villain. The bare ar and legs seem almost about to twitch into life, so strong the feeling of actuality they convey. Kōshirō's Magoem has an air of dignity, seriousness, and restraint that sugge he will get the better of Hachiemon in any encounter.

78

55. *Matsumoto Yonesaburō as Otsuyu the maid* ◆ *hoso-ban* ◆ Tokyo National Museum ◆ This print apparently forms a set along with those shown in Plates 53 and 54, but it is so fine artistically that it seems preferable to enjoy it by itself. Particularly fine is the feeling, so common in Sharaku, that a single rod of some flexible material runs unseen through the figure from head to foot, together with an economical use of line and simple areas of flat color that create an impressive sense of scale and solidity. The composition of the upper half of the figure is also striking, depending as it does on a number of triangles piled on top of each other.

56. *Ichikawa Komazō II as Kameya Chūbei and Nakayama Tomisaburō as Umegawa* ◆ *ōban* ◆ mica-dust background ◆ Tokyo National Museum ◆ This illustrates the scene between the ill-starred lovers Chūbei and Umegawa— danced to voice and samisen accompaniment —that occurred at the end of *Katsura-gawa Tsuki no Omoide.* The whole effect, with the lovers in their matching kimono under a large umbrella, is typical of the kabuki's taste for the tragically romantic, interpreted in terms of an unrealistic beauty. The dark silver mica-dust background—this is the only one of Sharaku's twin-figure prints to use it—effectively enhances the prevailing mood.

80

Nakamura Noshio II as Ono no Komachi ◆ hosoban ◆ Naka-
Shin'ichirō collection

58. Sawamura Sōjūrō III as Ōtomo no Kuronushi ◆ hosoban ◆
Tokyo National Museum

e two prints form a set together with another of Kikunojō
ronushi's wife, Hanazono Gozen, which is placed on the
Both the characters are poets whose work occurs in the
ial anthology, *Kokinshū*, compiled in the tenth century,
he bundle of wood that Kuronushi carries, as well as the

basin of water placed by Komachi's side, are witty references to
famous stories associated with the two poets. Noshio was an
actor who came to Edo from Osaka around this time, and his
face as portrayed here suggests that Sharaku may have referred
to the type of picture then popular in the Osaka-Kyoto area.

59. *Nakamura Nakazō II as Aramaki Mimishirō Kanetora posing as Saizō* ◆ *hosoban* ◆ The Art Institute of Chicago, Buckingham Collection of Japanese Prints

60. *Segawa Kikunojō III as the dancer Hisakata posing as Yan Manzai* ◆ *hosoban* ◆ on loan to the Tokyo National Museum

The prints are of two characters in *Ōshukubai Koi no Hatsun* dance number that occurs within the main play. Both prints large-scale works, full of life; in fact, the impressive bearing beautiful form of the figure of Kikunojō, together with the wit urgent vitality of that of Nakazō put them at the head of Sharak print groups of this period.

紀伊國屋納子

寫樂画

61. *Sawamura Sōjūrō III as Kujaku Saburō* ◆ *aiban* ◆ Kodaka Chū
collection ◆ A loyal retainer of Prince Korehito, here apparently
in the garb of a courier, Sōjūrō's facial expression and the soft,
unemphatic quality of his movements are skillfully captured in
this work. But compared with his appearances in Sharaku's earlier
prints he seems somehow to have diminished in stature.

62. *Segawa Kikunojō III as the maid Ohama* ◆ *aiban* ◆ The
Art Institute of Chicago, Buckingham Collection of Japanese
Prints ◆ This character is in fact the wife of the villain of the
piece, posing as a maid in a geisha house in order to further
her husband's schemes. The way the body is twisted creates a
sense of movement, and the composition as a whole is well
organized.

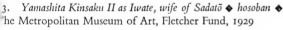

63. *Yamashita Kinsaku II as Iwate, wife of Sadatō* ◆ *hosoban* ◆
The Metropolitan Museum of Art, Fletcher Fund, 1929

64. *Ichikawa Yaozō III as Saeki Kurando Tsunenori* ◆ *hosoban*
◆ The Art Institute of Chicago, Buckingham Collection of
Japanese Prints

These two prints may not have been intended as a pair, but
these two actors do in fact appear together, and in their composition the two prints seem to complement each other. The
figure of Yaozō accurately captures a moment of vigorous
action, while the plump, crouching form of Kinsaku has an
inner resilience that is echoed by the curving form of the plum
tree in the background.

65. *Ichikawa Yaozō III as Gengo Narishige posing as Hachiman Tarō Yoshiie* ◆ *hosoban* ◆ The Metropolitan Museum of Art, Rogers Fund, 1936

66. *Ichikawa Ebizō as Abe no Sadatō posing as Kagenari, Kamakura no Gondayū* ◆ *hosoban* ◆ Fogg Art Museum, Harvard University

These two prints, which obviously form a pair, are believed to represent the scene in which Kagenari arrives as an envoy from the shogun. There is an exchange between the two men, at the end of which Kagenari, pretending that he is about to commit suicide, stabs Hachiman Tarō to death instead and reveals himself to be Abe no Sadatō. The figure of Narishige, entering with measured tread, well conveys the majesty and mystery of kabuki.

86

天王子屋里虹

寫樂画

67. *Yamashita Kinsaku II as Iwate, wife of Sadatō, posing as the maid Ebizō Okane* ◆ *aiban* ◆ Boston Museum of Fine Arts, Spaulding Collection ◆ Other sources refer to this role as the daughter of Sadatō, but the *ehon banzuke* clearly states that she is his wife. The work is particularly famous among the *aiban* half-length portraits for the unusual expression of the face. Unfortunately, an unusual expression does not necessarily make for great art. The actor had come to Edo from Osaka, and it seems possible that in producing this work, Sharaku had reference to pictures of the same actor appearing in, for example, the picture books of Ryūkōsai.

87

68. *Ichikawa Danjūrō VI as Arakawa Tarō* ◆ *aiban* ◆ The Art Institute of Chicago, Buckingham Collection of Japanese Prints ◆ The *ehon banzuke* lists this role as played by Ichikawa Omezō, but apparently Danjūrō took over at short notice on account of the death, the previous month, of Omezō's father Monnosuke. The print manages to suggest the youth and spirit of the actor, who was only seventeen at the time.

88

akata Hangorō III as Abumizuri no Iwazō the groom ◆ hoso-
The Art Institute of Chicago, Buckingham Collection of
se Prints

70. *Yamashita Kinsaku II as Sadatō's wife Iwate* ◆ *hosoban* ◆ Boston
Museum of Fine Arts, Spaulding Collection

These prints are probably a pair, since both have a snowy background. Kinsaku, a stout *onnagata* originally from Osaka, is portrayed with a splendid economy of line, and the print gives an
enormous sense of solidity. Hangorō's pose is also captured with
considerable skill.

89

71. *Nakayama Tomisaburō as Teriha, sister of Abe no Sadatō, posing as Ohisa, wife of Sasanami Tatsugorō* ◆ *hosoban* ◆ Louis Hill, Jr. collection ◆ In *The Surviving Works of Sharaku* by Henderson and Ledoux, and in T. Yoshida's works, this character is described as Ohide, but if the *ehon banzuke* and *yakuwari banzuke* are to be believed, it is obviously Ohisa. Apparently the print shows a scene in which Ohisa engages in a struggle, acted out in pantomime, with two male characters. The upper half of the body is skillfully done, but the lower half is perfunctory.

72. *Ichikawa Ebizō as Abe no Sadatō posing as the pilgrim Ryō hosoban* ◆ Boston Museum of Fine Arts, Bigelow Collect The way the figure is shown confidently barring the way, wi sword eased a few inches out of the "pilgrim's staff" in whic concealed, skillfully conveys the impressive stage presence particular actor.

73. *Matsumoto Kōshirō IV as Hata Rokurōzaemon Tokinori posing as Minagawa Shinzaemon the Boatman* ◆ *hosoban* ◆ C. H. Mitchell collection

74. *Iwai Hanshirō IV as Sakurai, sister of Kusunoki Masashige, posing as Otoma* ◆ *hosoban* ◆ The Art Institute of Chicago, Buckingham Collection of Japanese Prints

These are two prints from a set of four showing a scene in which Shinzaemon and another force their way into Otoma's house with an eye to winning her hand. Both prints suffer from the crudity of the line.

75. *Ichikawa Monnosuke II* ◆ *aiban* ◆ Tokyo National Museum

76. *Nakajima Mioemon II and Nakamura Tomijūrō* ◆ *aiban* ◆ Tokyo National Museum

These two prints, made in memory of Monnosuke, who died in the tenth month of 1794, form a pair. The costumes and composition are suggested by a scene from the well-known play *Shibaraku,* but here Mioemon, on the right, is shown as king of the underworld, while the newly arrived Monnosuke has just fought and defeated two demons. The weird atmosphere of the right-hand picture contrasts well with the heroics of that on the left.

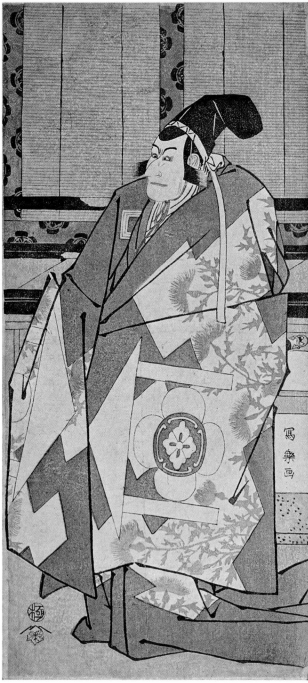

77. *Ichikawa Danjūrō VI as Soga no Gorō Tokimune* ◆ *hoso-ban* ◆ Boston Museum of Fine Arts, Spaulding Collection

78. *Ichikawa Ebizō as Kudō Saemon Suketsune* ◆ *hosoban* ◆ Bostoɪ Museum of Fine Arts, Spaulding Collection

In the "confrontation scene," the Soga brothers' enemy Kudō was not a despicable villain, but a man of commanding presence, and was usually played by the head of the troupe. Despite the weakness of the line in Sharaku's last prints, the majesty of Ebizō is well captured here, and Danjūrō, as he edges toward Ebizō, has a great sense of strength. A third print should stand to the left.

94

79. *The Wrestler Daidōzan Bungorō at the Age of Eight* ◆ *ai-ban* ◆ Tokyo National Museum ◆ The famous wrestler, still too young to have had the tucks taken out of his kimono shoulders, is using a massive *go* (Japanese checkers) board in order to put out a candle. The subject is interesting, but there is little depth in the treatment.

80. *Ichikawa Ebizō as Takemura Sadanoshin* ◆ *ōban* ◆ mica-dust background ◆ Takahashi Sei-ichirō collection ◆ Ebizō was unrivaled among the actors of his day in technical ability and majesty of bearing. The role of Sadanoshin is a tragic one, a Nō actor who is driven to commit suicide because of his daughter's disgrace. The face is full of character, with the deep lines, the penetrating eyes, and the set of the mouth that suggests the resonant voice of the actor, and the clenched fist resting on the hand at the point where the folds of the kimono sweep down and meet each other forms a pivot on which the whole weight of the picture seems to hinge. The work passes beyond mere exaggeration to achieve a striking psychological truth.

96